SIRPETER'S LAWS
OF NIGERIAN
POLITICS

SIRPETER'S LAWS OF NIGERIAN POLITICS

8 Laws that Guarantee Political Success in Nigeria

Ùgòchúkwú Àlòh

Copyright © 2020 Ùgòchúkwú Àlòh

ISBN: 979-8-8959-4479-2

To order additional copies of this book, contact:

Website: sirpeteraloh.com
Amazon.com
WhatsApp: +2347065972984
Email: sirpeteraloh@gmail.com

DEDICATION

I would like to dedicate this book to the Not Too Young to Run Movement and all the youths who want to run for political office in Nigeria. Your protests and participation have widened Nigeria's political space.

TABLE OF CONTENTS

ACKNOWLEDGEMENT

THE seed of this BOOK may have been sown years ago when I started my political philosophy journey but its realization WOULD have not been possible without the phenomenal support of a number of people.

First among them and quite incomparable with any human subject is the God of my Knowledge, *Deus scientiarum Dominus,* the Almighty God without whom I know nothing but through whom I can do all things. Next, I appreciate my family, the uniquely unquantified sacrifices of my mom, the immeasurable influence of my dad, the delightful communion I share with my brothers, and the spectacular bond I enjoy with my sisters.

I want to express as well my gratitude to my editor, Osinakachi Akuma Kalu. Even before I ran for office, it was Osinakachi's incredible suggestion that led me to document my experiences. At each stage of my political career, he has been encouraging, assisting, promoting and charitable with his time despite his numerous engagements. In a single phrase, Osinakachi is an ideal friend and a remarkable editor. His support was thoroughly boosted by the incredible assistance of Augustus Chukwu who despite my tendency to unload my worries to him has uncountable times accommodated my discussions, giving me better insights, and refining my ideas to be as excellent as they can be.

A number of journalists whose editorial and writing skills gave me insights cannot escaped being mentioned: Simon Kolawole, Akin Osuntokin, Reuben Abatti, Segun Adeniyi, Chidi Amuta, Shaka Momodu, Dele Momodu and Alex Otti. Their diagnosis about Nigeria's political affairs are deep and their prognosis of our trajectory as a nation are most times correct. Next in line are my lecturers who in the words of Albert Schweitzer "lighted the flame within me", deserved of special mention are: Profs., Izu Marcel Onyeocha, Ejiogu Amaku, Philip Ogbonna, George Ekwuru, Francis Njoku and Drs. Chrysanthus Ogbozo, Nicholas Mbogu,, Steve Oguji, Omenuko Donald, Elias Nwokeke and Emmanuel Ukata. I want to single out the sterling Professor of political science, Prof. Ian Shapiro who taught me the Moral Foundation of Politics from Yale University. It's not every student that has the opportunity to meet incredible teachers who are devoted to enlightening the young ones in wisdom and knowledge. No one confronts such teachers and remain the same. The reality is that I can never thank you enough but you all have my lifelong appreciation.

Worthy of mention are my heroes, Martin Luther King Jr., Mohandas Gandhi, Nelson

Mandela, Kofi Annan, Peter Obi and Barack Obama. I owe a special thanks to my mentors—Dr. Chidi Ogbuta, and Mr. Ugochukwu Omeogu. Thanks to them, I have learned to always go beyond the the call of duty to find more ways to always add value in people's lives. Your support, advice and suggestions have minimized my mistakes and maximized my progress towards my vision, and for that I am tremendously grateful.

Finally, I want to thank my team, who together we toured several parts of my constituency in caravan like kind of campaign. Your dedication and sacrifices made a world of difference. Special of mention is my personal assistant, Theophilus Odu, in you I found a friend, and a brother.

You all are much involved in my success of this book just as I am. Sure you have this book in your hands, but it couldn't have happened without these certain key players. They held me to the standard of my goal even to a higher one, despite their busy schedule. Thank you so much.

FOREWORD

Plato once said, "One of the penalties of refusing to participate in politics is that you end up being governed by your inferiors." This is indisputably true. I had the singular honour of knowing Ùgòchúkwú Àlòh for several years now. He is a passionate individual with an unusual devotion to humanitarian causes, social-political activism, and global issues.

Sirpeter's Laws of Nigerian Politics is quite a politically enlightening and insightful book that touches on the heart of Nigerian politics. The author painstakingly distilled and analyzed the important factors that are valuable to anyone who wants to successfully make an enroute into Nigerian politics and other third world countries. The laws are not mere theoretical postulations but concrete variables coming from a scholar in humanity who have had practical experience in Nigerian politics.

Albeit, the colouration of those factors, he also admonished young people to venture into politics for as John Donne says In his Immortal poem, "never send to know for whom the bell tolls: It tolls for thee." This is not to scare readers but only to uncover key cardinals of the current Nigerian politics. No doubt politics all over the World has its ugly sides, but it is too much an important affair to be left at the hands of charlatans, deplorables, and wolfers, and since God cannot come down from heaven and change our polity, we need good men in the political field. As the author rightly opined, politics is not for saints but for earthly performers. Therefore, we need good and excellent workmen in Africa to change the fortunes of the continent not necessarily saints.

Furthermore, to make a measurable impact in this current African political setting, it demands the dialectic of our idealism and realism. Politics entails compromise especially here in Nigeria, but you can still bend without being defiled. It entails a lot of sophistication. The nitty-gritty is to get prepared, play your cards well to get there, and change the narrative for good; this is the message the author is desirous to convey to you in this sublime piece.

Orji Ama Chinedu (Esq)

Lagos

6th October, 2020

The only thing necessary for the triumph of evil is for good men to do nothing —

EDMUND BURKE

Introduction

More than twenty-seven years ago, I was born in one of the greatly impaired maternities of Ebonyi State, Nigeria. My village just like many villages in Nigeria is one of the most dangerous places to give birth on earth. I could have died like the 262,000 babies who die at birth every year in Nigeria, but thanks to the diligent efforts of our underpaid and sometimes owed healthcare workers, I survived.

When I was 3 years old, I enrolled in nursery and primary school where I began my formal education. Due to the financial situation of my parents who struggle to put food on the table, and worsened by lack of social security, I with some of my friends would pluck mangoes and guavas along the way to school to substitute for the breakfast we didn't have before coming to school.

Many at times, we were late to school because we had to wake up early in the morning to trek a long distance to fetch water in far away borehole with a long queue of people seeking for the same water. Along the way, I managed to take my First School leaving certificate examination and enrolled in a secondary school not different from the primary school I attended.

With broken walls and patched roofs, poor desks, and inadequate teachers which are trademarks of public schools in Nigeria, my studies were hindered but I was undaunted. I managed to graduate from secondary school with my SSCE. Upon graduation, I worked in a milling firm where I got firsthand experience of how difficult it is for my parents and many other families to put a meal on the table for their kids. I had to wake up as early as 3—4 am to grind the beans, maize, millet, and other cereals which these families had to hawk sometimes in the morning of harmattan or terrible rainfall just to make ends meet.

Convinced of my passion to help humanity, I sought admission to study Medicine at a University. One of my uncles said that since I didn't study in a special science school and that my scientific foundation is poor already, it will be difficult to adjust to medical paraphernalia in school. And worse still there's no money to pay for high school fees. He counseled me to be less ambitious and go to a polytechnic.

Though I didn't agree with him, I went on to buy the JAMB and Post-Utme form of Federal Polytechnic Nekede, where I got admitted to study Science Laboratory Technology. But owing to the fact that the course actually wasn't what I wanted,

I declined to study and instead volunteered for the priesthood. In the seminary, for close to two years, I served both as a procurator and infirmarian. My entire mission consisted of purchasing goods for the feeding of minor seminarians and taking care of the sick ones in the hospital often in vulnerable conditions.

Afterwards, I enrolled for my Undergraduate Studies at Claretian Institute of Philosophy Maryland Nekede (CIP), an affiliate of Imo State University Owerri and Pontifical Urban University Rome, and I found a new vision and purpose. In CIP, which doubles as a seminary, I began a quest for knowledge with a humanitarian disposition; I learned how intense and sustained study with disciplined conversation help in understanding and analyzing a whole range of issues with proper clarifications in order to arrive at creative solutions.

Yet, whenever I travel to visit an uncle, came to my village for holidays, or see the numerous out of school children roaming our streets, or lurking around motor parks asking for anything from anyone going anywhere or elderly women felling into ditches as they go to farm, or young teen girls being heavily pregnant, or hospitals rejecting patients because of lack of bed space, I feel terribly bad. And I wondered unexplainably: What crime does one commit by being born in an underdeveloped country?

Trouble by this state of affairs, I studied deeply the cause of social justice, democracy, rule of law, etc. I immersed myself in books of men like Martin Luther King Jr., Barack Obama, Nnamdi Azikiwe, Awolowo, Olusegun Obasanjo, Nelson Mandela, Kwame Nkrumah, Leopold Senghor, Chinua Achebe, Wole Soyinka, Goodluck Jonathan to mention but a few. And their ideas further inflamed my passion for social justice. And I began to espouse my stance through social media and radio presentations on how the youths can bury the corrosive petty partisan politics in Nigeria.

The responses I got from my radio discussions and social media posts, made me understand as never before, that young people want something better for themselves. I recognized we want to live more in alignment with our dreams for a better family, healthcare, housing, education, and job. We want to be more in control of our lives and to experience good transformations in our country.

Fortunately, my school is one of those 'mini ivy league' institutions that celebrate the elevation of the spirit of man as God's masterpiece who has the responsibility of making places and persons better than they found them. Most of my professors didn't just teach philosophy, they brought its practical relevance in the lives of men, women, and children to my awareness. They epitomized the fervor of someone implanting a seed in fertile soil to bear fruit— 'fruits that will last.'

Imbued with enthusiasm and a heightened sensitivity to political and social justice, I burned with zeal to make a change and forged an agreement with my deepest self, that I will be dedicated—no devoted to leaving everyone I meet better than I found them and making my country and the world better than I was born in it. During my graduate year, I wrote a memoir titled, "Ockham's Razor: A Paradigm for Socio-Political Development in Nigeria", in which I investigated why Nigeria has not joined the league of developed nations, irrespective of her numerous human and natural resources. I found the answer in the fact that we wasted our resources in all the three arms of government due to superfluous policies, projects, and programs that have contributed to the ignoble current state of the Nigerian nation.

I, therefore, suggested reorienting Nigeria's socio-political affairs from being misdirected by superfluity, wastefulness, and glamorous lifestyle of unnecessary luxury to being orchestrated towards the need to address fundamental issues concerning the common good.

With a glimpse of these perceptions, it was impossible for me to remain a bystander to injustice, to be a mere spectator as things degenerate, to look the other way round as things got worse in the political arena. In any case, it was an effect of that inner turmoil that I decided to challenge a sitting PDP State House of Assembly members two months after my graduation from philosophy. Policy-wise, I was excellently prepared, with manifesto programs and ten-point plans whose arc is directly pointed towards the common good. But strategy-wise I was ill-equipped.

On the 9th of December 2018, I flew to Abuja for the "Not too young to run" conference organized by YIAGA Africa and sponsored by UKAID. About 400 youth candidates in the 2019 elections were invited. This number was possible because of the passage of the Not Too Young to Rule (NTYTR) Act signed into law on 31st May 2018 by President Buhari which made an alteration in sections 65, 106, 131, 177 of the Federal Republic of Nigeria Constitution, reducing the age for elective positions for House of Assembly and House of Representatives from 30 years to 25 years, Senate and Governorship from 35 years to 30 years and office of the president from 40 to 30 years and introduced independent candidature in Nigeria.

During the conference, I was able to network with several participants and we discussed strategies to win the election. Little did I know we were progressing in error. And after the election, I called several youth candidates, and awfully, several of them lost like myself. It dawned on me that while the NTYTR Act has given more youths the opportunity to contest elections in Nigeria, it has not given them the strategies to win elections in Nigeria. This book is designed to fill that gap.

This is because the dark forces that propel Nigeria's bad political culture are not about to retire. Nor are the merchants of political mediocrity going on vacation soon. Ensconced in political power with attached rewards of indescribable luxury that are sequestered from the hardships that appear to have numbed the supposed vociferous masses, these politicians defensively indulge in self-induced amnesia and byzantine superfluity. And in case you don't know the damage these people have done, as at the time of writing this, Apple, the American tech company now has the capacity to buy Nigeria as a country four times over. The recent evaluation of Apple is over $2 trillion. By contrast, the GDP of Nigeria is estimated at $448 billion.

What am I driving at? This book is a polite reminder that if youths continue to remain on the sidelines while these old people in the corridors of power sabotage our future; that if we allow these backward thinkers whose understanding of progress and prosperity is built around looting of the country resources, stashing it in silos, or ferrying cash abroad for foreign investment, history won't deliver a benign verdict to us at all.

If you know the damage these politicians have done to you and me, and to future generations unborn, you will know they don't deserve to be in office for another day. They have killed our educational system, stifled innovation, stunted our growth, corrupted our democracy, weakened our institutions, and destroyed the values our different traditional societies have in common. They have further polarised us along ethnic and religious lines and created a seemingly unbridgeable gap between governance and the poor masses. Nigerian Googles, Amazons, Facebooks, Apples, Samsungs, and Microsofts remain unconceived, suffer miscarriages, or become stillborn — because these people refused to invest in education.

- You generate your electricity and pay high tariff for the one that is rarely provided
- You provide your water by sinking your own boreholes
- You fix the roads yourself with stones
- You shoulder your education as a student by doing menial works
- You provide your own job by creating SME's that's overtaxed
- You pay taxes and receive no social security in return

Basically, we have a government in perpetual retreat and retrogressive backwardness. And you continue to fill up the void practically from scratch. It was Chinua Achebe who in his small but powerful book, *The Trouble With Nigeria* described the story of Nigeria so perfectly that you would think he wrote it today whereas he wrote it nearly 37 years ago. It goes thus:

"I believe there are individuals as well as nations who, on account of peculiar gifts and circumstances, are commandeered by history to facilitate mankind's advancement. Nigeria is such a nation. The vast human and material wealth with which she is endowed bestows on her a role in Africa and the world which no one else can assume or fulfill. The fear that should nightly haunt our leaders (but does not) is that they may already have betrayed irretrievably Nigeria's high destiny. The countless billions that a generous Providence poured into our national coffers in the last ten years (1972-1982) would have been enough to launch this nation into the middle-rank of developed nations and transformed the lives of our poor and needy. But what have we done with it? Stolen and salted away by people in power and their accomplices. Squandered in uncontrolled importation of all kinds of useless consumer merchandise from every corner of the globe. Embezzled through inflated contracts to an increasing army of party loyalists who have neither the desire nor the competence to execute their contracts. Consumed in the escalating salaries of a grossly overstaffed and unproductive public service. And so on ad infinitum."

Not done, Achebe then posed a haunting question:

"Does it ever worry us that history which neither personal wealth nor power can pre-empt will pass terrible judgment on us, pronounce anathema on our names when we have accomplished our betrayal and passed on? We have lost the twentieth century; are we bent on seeing that our children also lose the twenty-first?"

To put it mildly, Nigeria is suffering from a deficit of leaders. We need leaders, pure leaders, and not narcissists obsessed with their own self-interests at the detriment of the common good. Our journey from underdevelopment to development will continue to be halted unless we have leaders who know and act on the knowledge that our best resources are our human resources. We need leaders who can focus on creating an enabling and productive environment, where businesses and citizens can flourish. Because any leader whose loyalty is to his pocket ought to be cast aside while those who prioritize human development should step in.

In Nigeria since the fourth republic, during every election cycle with exception of variation of some states, we have an estimated total of over 11,607 elective positions. There are at any given time, the President, Vice President, 109 Senators, 360 House of Representative members 36 Governors, 36 Deputy governors, about 1,000 plus members of state houses of assembly, 776 Local government chairmen, and 9,288 Councilors.

Now, you do not need to be a political philosopher or scientist to know that Nigerians suffer from poverty and degeneration of governance. But the admonition of Chidi Amuta bears relevance, "Since 1999, democracy has delivered two persisting dividends to Nigeria: a predictable calendar of national ritual and a gigantic all-powerful political industry. Imperfections and disfigurements notwithstanding, we now have a fair idea of what must happen in this polity every four years. The campaigns. The festival of rallies. The pageant of politicians who address mobs of starving illiterates in English. The parade of known villains as born again messiahs crowned by the reduction of our national hopes into party marketing slogans and lazy catchphrases. Afterwards, the mournful processions of losers and their crashing ambitions drowned by the drums of triumph and ascension trails of winners to power, wealth, and glory."[1]

Though we have had a few honest political actors who have however come close to serving the people in their short stints in political leadership.

But the deficiency of true leaders is outrageous and the need is imminent. When you deconstruct how successful nations are built and you reflect at the current trajectory of Nigeria, you will understand that Nigeria is bound to remain a perpetual potentially great nation, unless responsible leadership is exercised.

Now look at the drama of Niger Delta Development Commission (NDDC) and the National Assembly, to that of governors who empower their citizens to be Mai shai tea and egg sellers or those who deceive the First-Class Graduates of their states with phantom jobs existing only in his illusion, to senators who commission wheelbarrows, motorcycles, POS centers in the name of constituency projects.

For all that they are worth, these insulting projects that do not connect to the people's need amount to a tragic betrayal of trust in leadership positions. More specifically, the insolent impunity is an egregious abuse of the integrity of the Office which they occupy and a gross devaluation of the sanctity of a union that represents the collective will of Nigerians.

What we have mostly in Nigeria's Presidency, and the 36 States, with few exceptions, is a massive casino of corruption and an infinite bazaar of dubious deals and callous contracts. Power in Nigeria has become a ticket to join in the largest heist that exists and has continued to exist in the history of humanity.

But all inanities and betrayals have their limits. As Hassan Kukah says, "The youth have enough weapons to destroy this treacherous heist from its very foundation." The buck must stop somewhere. And it begins with the mirrors in all our houses as we ask ourselves pertinent questions:

Why is it that the qualifications to scale through our leadership recruitment process are violence, vote-buying, and black-market judgments?

Why would the common treasury become the piggy bank of a progression of looters, each successor determining to loot more than his predecessor?

Why must the worst and the foolish of us represent the best and the brightest?

How can a simple duty of providing oversight be degenerated to a gigantic serial fraud?

How has an annual ritual of passing a budget be turned into an exercise of padding fraudulent projects and dubious contracts?

How can a single commission create to alleviate the suffering of those who produce the "National cake" be a massive hemorrhaging of the treasury to the committee members ONLY to the detriment of those it was created for?

How can a supposed conclave of the representatives of Nigerians interest become easily one of the most coordinated corruption coalitions in the world?

The tragedy is that unless those who know how to connect with the needs of the people occupy leadership positions or those who in leadership positions learn how to connect with the needs of the people, Nigeria is bound never to relinquish its unenviable reputation of being the poverty epicenter of the world. And substantially degrade to a Hobbesian state of nature where life is brutish, short, and miserable.

And as a student of power politics who spent several years studying Nigerian politics and partaking in it, I have distilled my findings into eight basic laws that govern success and failure in Nigerian politics. Violate them at your own risk, utilize them at your own gain. I began documenting my observations of countless politicians right from my undergraduate days of philosophy. I uncovered books, Newspapers, blogposts orthogonally in alignment with Nigerian politics. In the process, I found out that there are a set of distilled laws that can help good-willed individuals who want to partake in Nigeria's politics.

Notwithstanding, different individuals use divergent methodologies to achieve victory in Nigeria's politics, but I found out that there are commonalities behind the winners of the polls that are conspicuously missing among the losers. My job here is to give the facts. It's your business and your responsibility for how you interpret them.

So, this will be a book of ruthless pragmatism and stories from Nigeria's history that illustrate the potency of these laws. It teaches you how to play the game of power politics with only one end in mind—victory for the sake of achieving the common good. As Timothy Snyder
Says, "Life is political, not because the world cares about how you feel, but because the world reacts to what you do."[2]

Seek ye first the kingdom of money and everything else shall be added unto it! —
Dele Momodu

CHAPTER ONE

FIRST LAW

Money is the substructure, structure, and superstructure of Nigerian politics. People vote according to the size of their greed not according to their hunger for development. In fact, seek ye first the kingdom of money and electoral victory shall be added unto it. The reality of the Nigerian political environment is such that, the people are after their belly than their future; they prioritize the short term over the long term and those who architect the machinery of the state understand this law.

Politics in Nigeria is all about money on all sides. Election time is an opportunity for everyone involved in the election value-chain to make money. Poverty and ignorance have been incorporated and integrated into the lives of the people such that any amount of money will buy their loyalty and votes.

I had this peculiar experience on the campaign trail, such that everywhere I went, I was asked to "drop money". Not even the youths were interested in the bills I proposed to sponsor. I talked endlessly with few people listening about our being the poorest people in the world, our impassable roads, rising teen pregnancy, ever-increasing hoodlums, cultism, drug abuse by the youths, our numerous out of school children, and the non-existent health care for the aged. Many were not listening because I was not sharing money, not because I wasn't addressing the issues correctly.

This frightening poverty, I witnessed in the lives of the people has led to a total collapse of human dignity and values. Right in your face people will tell you I will only vote for the candidate who gives me money, even after you've analyzed the uselessness of the N500 ($1.5) they receive on election day. At drinking bars, you will be asked to pay the bills for drinks. At wedding ceremonies, you will have to donate hugely.

At churches, you will be expected to contribute to projects. Literally, everyone you meet will expect you to "drop something", "facilitate", "mobilize" and several other words people use as synonyms for you to give them money, because they believe that once you're elected, you will forget them. And that seems a good reason for they have been betrayed endlessly by successive politicians to the point that they have no hope even when an angel comes.

This is a general phenomenon. According to Reuben Abati—Deputy Governorship Candidate, "I was asked to pick up bills at drinking joints. People stopped by and asked for money to "enjoy the rest of the evening". Others came with requests for money to pay hospital fees, to take care of a newly born baby, to bury a relative, or to make a girlfriend happy. One political associate told me that every request was valid because as far as the Nigerian people are concerned, only a thief goes into politics and it is better to "take their own share" before the election.[3]

Kingsley Moghalu, the Presidential Candidate for Young Progressive Party confirmed his own experience when he said, "The 2019 elections were marred by an orgy of vote-buying, rigging, vote-suppression and violence, all superintended by the chaotic operations of the Independent National Electoral Commission (INEC). Voting at my polling unit in Nnewi North LGA, my home town, opened three hours late as a result of card reader malfunction. At some point, the card readers failed again. Voting went on manually, against INEC regulations. I observed that there was no privacy for the ballot boxes, so anyone milling around behind a voter could potentially see his or her voting choices. The "business" of vote-buying proceeded merrily apace in a corner of the voting premises. From several states around the country, we received credible reports that votes cast for the Young Progressives Party (YPP), my party platform for the 2019 elections, were being diverted."[4]

During the primaries, major political parties fix very high and outrageous sums of money as the price for presidential nomination form and expression of interest to contest. For the APC, in 2015, the presidential expression of interest and nomination form amounted to N27.5m (N25m for the nomination form and N2.5m for expression of interest). For the PDP, the sum of N22m (N20m for the form and N2m for expression of interest) was required for the same purpose.[5]

In primary elections, most delegates vote for the candidates that offer the highest amount of cash. For instance, the over 8,000 delegates who participated in the APC presidential primary in Lagos state before the 2015 elections allegedly made US$5,000 each from the candidates, just for the three days of the primaries. Delegates were supposed to have received US$2,000 each from the Atiku Abubakar group and also US$3,000 each from the Buhari group.[6] During PDP National Convention in 2018, some delegates claim to receive $9,000 each from different candidates.[7]

The extant Electoral Act (2010) in Nigeria is very specific about campaign finance and the exact amount that a politician is allowed to raise and spend to seek particular offices. The law states that a presidential candidate can only spend a maximum amount of N1 billion, a governorship candidate, N200 million, a senatorial candidate, N40 million, House of Representatives candidate, N20 million, State House of Assembly, N10 million, chairman of local government, N10 million, and councilorship, N1 million.

But these campaign finance regulations are meaningless in Nigerian elections. The aspirants and candidates spend money as they like, the supposed regulatory authorities look the other way, before, during, and after elections. In 2011, the total traceable expenses of the PDP were a little over N5 billion and those of three opposition parties (ACN, APGA, and CPC) combined was just above N2 billion. However, in 2015, the total traceable amount expended by the PDP increased to almost N9 billion. The APC expended almost N3 billion naira in the same year.[8]

Some candidates sell their houses, vehicles, shares, and other possessions to be able to raise the needed money to campaign for office. Some even go to the extent of taking bank loans as Buhari did in 2015. Others like myself did rely on a network of family and friends to finance the exorbitant electoral process. But there is something common to them all: they incur debts ahead of the election. Should they be lucky enough to win, they have to settle those who brought them to power.[9]

The thing with this law of money in Nigeria politics is that it keeps rising with each successive election cycle. For example, candidates contesting to be president on the platform of the PDP in the 2007 general elections were each required to pay N10,000 for expression of interest forms and N5 million for nomination forms, a candidate for the house of representatives paid N10,000 for expression of interest form and N500,000 for nomination forms. However, for the 2015 general elections, presidential candidates were required to pay N2 million for expression of interest forms and N20 million for nomination forms. Candidates for the house of representatives are now required to pay N500,000 for expression of interest forms and N2 million for nomination forms.

Understand: In many ways, Nigerian politics is all about money. You can talk about the poverty index on the campaign trail, social media, radio, television, and in writing. You can quote statistics from the right sources. You can derive a manifesto for action on how to solve our numerous political problems, complete with charts and graphs, timetables, and ten-point plans but when you go onto the field of politics, you are bound to confront the reality of the poverty that has turned the Nigerian electorate into an endless congregation of beggars and cynics.

The tragedy of Nigeria is the impoverishment of the people and the total collapse of values and dignity. Almost in everything you do in Nigerian politics, people will beg, ask and even coerce you to give them money. They are not interested in programs or policies you are campaigning for, they may listen to you when you talk about development and progress, but that is after you have given them money. The reality is that Nigerian politicians have over the years destroyed the people's hopes. The political field is peopled by hypocrites who exploit the people's poverty and the citizens themselves have become dangerously cynical and monetized.[10]

Beware of this law, money is the substructure, structure, and superstructure of Nigerian politics. People vote according to the size of their greed not according to their hunger for development. This is not to support Nigerian excessively exploitative politics, or whitewash the evils of vote-buying, or high price for nomination forms of parties. Nope! I'm just stating the laws that you must utilize if you must get the opportunity of being elected. That doesn't mean you should compromise your core values—Justice, integrity, responsibility, care, etc. But you must deploy money in Nigerian politics If you want to get the opportunity to make things better. And from there you can consolidate your gains and move on to make a change from a stronger position.

*Politics is not a job
for heavenly saints
but of earthly
performers.*

— Ùgòchúkwú Àlòh

CHAPTER TWO

SECOND LAW

You must mesh political theories with Nigerian practicality and forfeit some of your idealism for ruthless realism. Compromise is a key to success in politics worldwide, but in Nigeria, you have to leave idealism in your study room and carry pragmatic flexibility into the battlefield, probably later if you win, you can excavate your idealism and pursue it to concrete realization.

If you are only thinking that politics is about campaign rallies and espousing of ideas, you're really mistaken. The democracy of Nigeria is not structured like the ones you read in books. "It is not a government of the people by the people and for the people". "We the people" in Nigerian democracy refers to "we the political elite". You must accept some compromise from people. You must accept the importance of even those you don't like, you must court the support of those you don't even respect, otherwise, you won't win. You must promise to do some of their bidding which most times may be in direct assault with the common good.

During my campaign, filled with idealism and moral purity, I reiterated to some youths that I don't facilitate people with drinks to vote for me, some youths resort to violent attacks. On one of my days of the campaign, I went to a drinking bar and I was asked to pick up their bills, I respectfully declined with the explanation that when we take inducements from politicians, you'll be forced to vote for them even if they're incompetent. Some picked offense and chased me and my campaign team away with bottles. Under the influence of the incumbents' drink and smoke, some youths tore my posters, forcefully seized the rest from my team, and set it ablaze. I told my team not to retaliate and we went to another area of my constituency to campaign.

This is because, the nobility of my intentions and vision, have led me to believe that when I entered the political scene it would be easy for me to espouse my ideas, convince people to buy into it and engage in implementing solutions to our problems. I thought my success is dependent on my goodwill. But with the hard experience I found out the bitter truth—Nigerian politics doesn't reward goodwill it rewards those who adhere to the rules of its game. And the success of any politics is reflected in the reality of what is obtainable in a particular environment. So goodwill and manifestoes don't deliver victory, mastery of the laws does.

Understand: There will always be a quid pro quo in politics! *Politics worldwide is not a job for heavenly saints but of earthly performers.* And in Nigeria specifically, though sadly, you cannot succeed without a mix of angels and evil men. To win, you must rise above religious sentimentalism and moralistic categorization. Politics in Nigeria is mostly amoral. The vendors of chronic vote-buying and incessant violence will strive to vitiate the aims of the politics of free and fair. In fact, in some situations, only the devil can protect you from evil, the angels will gladly run away when such situations occur.

If you believe that only Saints are what is needed to win elections in Nigeria, you are doomed to failure. There are cynics who believe that it's impossible to be a good man in Nigeria politics. For them, Nigeria can never be good, and "Only God" can save Nigeria. So they've resorted not to waste their time casting votes until God come down from heaven and contest Nigeria elections. This is highly discouraging. Let me repeat this because it's very important: politics is not a job for heavenly Saints but for earthly performers.

It suffices to say that, you won't know which group is more frustrating to engage in policy discussion—the "beggars" group looking for money or the cynical group who have lost all hope. While the "beggars" group ears are closed until you "drop money", the cynical group hearts are blocked until "God comes down". Both groups have "conditions" that are insatiable.

In one of my campaign days, I was accosted by a particular youth who belonged to one of those cults. He was threatening fire and brimstone and I have to honestly admit I was scared to my teeth. And I couldn't engage him in a battle of fists for I would be beaten to hell. I have always preached to my team the importance of nonviolence and so I allowed him to rant all he can, threatening me not to come and campaign in his area again, otherwise, he would deal with me.

Luckily passing by, was another member of a rival gang who suddenly came to my aid. He warned the guy not to threaten me again because I am from his own ward, and everyone is free to campaign anywhere. Knowing the notoriety of the person speaking and his infamy in the village of dealing with people ruthlessly, the young man capitulated and walked away. It was like "Taming of a shrew". I found out that the reason people will fear to hurt you is when they know the power of those who will come against them if they touch you.

But if you refuse to engage the so-called "devils" out of some sense of moral purity, then those your great ideas of development would just remain ideas. To bring about the change you want to see, you have to engage them. And that's how victory is achieved. Politics all over the world requires concession, even when you are 100 percent right, you must engage folks who disagree with you. But if you think that the only way forward is to be as uncompromising as possible, you may feel good about yourself, you will enjoy a certain sense of holiness, but you're not going to win and do the good you want. And if you don't get to do the good in your heart, you will eventually be more cynical and label 'politics a dirty game' leaving more vacuum in the system and since nature abhors a vacuum, corruption, injustice, prebendalism, ethnicism, will continue to fill the void and eventually pass to the next generations.

Remember there's nothing like a pure political party. Don't think you can import angels from heaven to take over the affairs of Nigeria. It was exactly discarding this mindset that catapulted Buhari to the President of Nigeria in 2015, when he had to engage with Tinubu, Amaechi, Atiku, etc., all of who had corruptions allegations on their head. In previous years he contested with only those he felt aligned with him on a moral standard, victory eluded him.

When you add religion to illiteracy plus politics, you just created a worse weapon than hydrogen bomb at a much cheaper cost. —

Goodluck Jonathan

CHAPTER THREE

THIRD LAW

You must learn to deploy ignorance to your own favour. Make no mistake about it, Nigeria is suffering from anti-intellectualism. Pretend you are one of the people, no matter the height of your level of intellectual development. The weaponization of ignorance has made your biggest enemies to come from those you're fighting to save.

This terrible situation successive administrations have kept Nigerians is captured aptly by the great African-American social reformer and abolitionist, Frederick Douglass, which explains our slavery and lack of educational liberation. He says, "To make a contented slave, you must make a thoughtless one. It's necessary to darken his moral and mental mission, and, as far as possible, to annihilate his power of reason. He must be able to detect no inconsistencies in slavery. The man that takes his earnings, must be able to convince him that he has a perfect right to do so. It must not depend upon mere force; the slave must know no Higher Law than his master's will. The whole relationship must not only demonstrate, to his mind, its necessity, but its absolute rightfulness."[11]

If you're a youth, be ready to be opposed by your fellow youths. If you're a woman, be ready to receive a tongue lashing from fellow women. (One of the women who ran for the office of governor received this remark from a fellow woman, "She—the woman candidate, thought that governorship election is beauty pageant contest") If you're a civil servant, your colleagues will mock you for leaving the comfort of financial security to go and waste your money. If you wish to succeed in Nigerian politics, you must find a way to utilize this law to serve your own ends.

Understand: Running successfully for office requires a thorough mixture of knowledge of where the country needs to be and an understanding of where the people are, so as to communicate to them in their own language. As the saying goes, when you go out to seek the lion's share of what belongs to all, you go in meekness.

Remember when you as a youth tell someone you want to run for office, the next thing they will tell you is you don't have money, you don't have charms, you're too young, you're unknown. Well, to be honest with you, if every youth waited for enough money to run for public offices in Nigeria, no youth will ever contest because the reality is, we can never get the amount required to contest. And so don't rely on intellectualism, know how to connect with people, because you have to deal with a lot of ignorance, hatred, ethnicism, foolishness, mockery. It won't be a fair fight with the cabals but you have to outwork them in a way that connects you to the ordinary man.

This law requires that you should be aware of self-appointed consultants and political strategists who are only after their pockets. Many of them will come to you. They will claim to know everything. They will tell you how they worked for that Governor and that Senator and how their strategies catapulted them to victory. Just be careful. Politics is about strategy, no doubt, but most Nigerian strategists that come during elections are fake. But no matter how fake you might find the things that come out of their mouths, don't try to shut them down, engage them but be strict with your pocket. And watch as they disappear into oblivion.

I was fooled severally by people who claim to know everything there's to know in politics. I had my own strategy based on a caravan like kind of campaign. These groups kept asking for money for every little thing. They wanted me to do big rallies like the incumbent who has a lot of money, but I declined and stuck with my strategy. After much persistence, I gave in. At the end of four rallies, I found out that these people are only interested in free food and money to buy drinks and smoke. They weren't even in support of my sharing exercise books to pupils and students of public schools, they were more devoted to sharing money and drinks at the rallies. And it was after the situation became financially unmanageable for me that my common sense seemed to come back. And I made known to them that I need volunteers who believe in the cause of development and progress of our constituency, not people who are interested only in food and drink, they naturally disappear when they saw they money wasn't flowing again.

But that's not a reason to be discouraged, just as the Holy Writ says, you are going like a sheep in the midst of wolves; so be wise as serpents and innocent as doves. It's something I know for a fact, the ignorance of the Nigerian citizenry cannot die, a set of people have to team up and kill it. If we don't, we will always be leaders of tomorrow by words of the mouth, never in reality.

So, you don't need more age. You don't need more money. You already have what it takes—the burning desire to make things better than they were and now the potency of these laws through its effective application. If you don't run for office, let it not be for what the ignorant critics told you, but out of a reasoned reflection on your vision and purpose and how you intend to achieve it. As Albert Einstein wrote 'Great spirits have always encountered violent opposition from mediocre minds. The mediocre mind is incapable of understanding the man who refuses to bow blindly to conventional prejudices and chooses instead to express his opinions courageously and honestly.'

And here's the sweetness of it all, you will have one of the best education on the campaign trail. I had one myself and spent some of the happiest moments during my caravan-like campaign especially from the students of various schools within my constituency. They are the ones who nominated me to run. Confronting them, I felt like I know next to nothing and I was reminded that learning is a lifelong commitment for any human who desires to make progress.

Among the children, I met where aeronauts that may never fly a plane, doctors that may never treat a disease, leaders that may never have an office, scholars that may never teach, writers that may never write, engineers that may never produce anything, entrepreneurs that may never found a business, all because there's no premium placed on education. As H.G. Wells said, "Human history becomes more and more a race between education and catastrophe". The abilities, the intelligence, the potentials of these young children have the tendency of remaining unharvested because the basics for development are conspicuously lacking. These are those I ran the office for and they taught me a lot.

*The political outcome of
Nigeria polls, reflecting
the continuing electoral
dominance of the APC
and PDP, points to the
mindset of our society at
this time.*

—Kingsley Moghalu

CHAPTER FOUR

FOURTH LAW

Without a mainstream political party, forget about being the President of Nigeria or governor of any of the 36 states of the federation. As Kingsley Moghalu puts it, "The political outcome of Nigeria polls, reflecting the continuing electoral dominance of the APC and PDP, points to the mindset of our society at this time."

Undoubtedly, millions and thousands of Nigerians will hear your message. Many will claim to love the message and the messenger. But for mushy reasons millions, including some of your advocates and initial supporters, will vote for the mainstream political parties. And in 2019, as Moghalu further avers, "they voted for the incumbent, President Muhammadu Buhari, and the PDP's Atiku Abubakar. Buhari voters wanted him to get a second term in office. Those opposed to him voted mainly for Atiku, "atikulating" the view that he was the only one who could take down the incumbent president. So, between the timing of our 2019 run and cynical voter calculations about the ability to win, vision, capacity, and policy prescriptions for real progress took second place."[12]

This is rightly true. The majority of opinion polls acknowledged that Buhari is nepotistic, insensitive, incompetent, tribalistic, and undemocratic. And that Atiku is corrupt, does shoddy deals, have a questionable source of riches. They acknowledged that both were evils but decided to vote for anyone they thought is the less of the two evils.

Many people further acknowledged that, Omoyele Sowore, Fela Durotoye, Kingsley Moghalu, or Tope Fasua are all competent, nationalistic, globally exposed, have the capacity, credibility, and know-how to move Nigeria to greater heights. But they don't believe any of those candidates can win the seat of the Nigerian presidency.

Yet some blamed the counting of the votes. They quoted the British playwright Tom Stoppard who said, "it's not the voting that is democracy, it's the counting" or Joseph Stalin similar statement, "The people who cast the votes decide nothing. The people who count the votes decide everything." Yes! INEC did a horrible betrayal of democracy in the way they conducted the election. The security agencies were highly complacent and collaborators to the riggers. No doubt, the 2019 general elections were marred by widespread fraud and defined by a debilitating combination of stultifying violence and INEC inefficiency. But people still gave those they acknowledged as "two evils" (who shunned national debate) 26 million votes while the summation of the credible candidates votes is not up to 1 million.

Let's look at the age of some of the youthful candidates for the Presidential race—Emmanuel Etim (38) of the Change Nigeria Party (CNP), Omoyele Sowore (47) of the African Action Alliance (AAC), Gbenga Olawepo-Hashim (49) of the People's Trust (PT), Kingsley Moghalu (55) of the Young Progressives Party (YPP, Ali Soyode (55) of the Yes Electorates Solidarity (YES), Olufunmilayo Adesanya-Davies (56) of the Mass Joint Action Alliance (MAJA), Adeshina Fagbenro-Byron (59) of the Kowa Party, Obadiah Mailafia (61) of the African Democratic Congress (ADC), Fela Durotoye (47) of the Alliance for New Nigeria (ANN), Tope Fasua (47) of the Abundant Nigeria Renewal Party (ANRP), Eunice Atuejide (40) of the National Interest Party (NIP).... Obiageli Ezekwesili (55) of the Allied Congress Party of Nigeria (ACPN).[13]

But for all these young minds and varied parties, the presidential election was reduced to a two-man, two-party race. A 76 –year old Muhammadu Buhari vs. a 72-year old Atiku Abubakar, PDP vs, APC. Anyways as the poet, John Greenleaf Whittier said, "For all sad words of tongue and pen, the saddest are these: 'It might have been'". It might have been Sowore, Moghalu, Fasua, Oby Ezekwesili, or Durotoye.

Understand: *To get a shot at the Nigerian presidency or governorship, you must join a mainstream political party, the idea of a third force is still far from the consciousness of the majority of Nigerian voters.*

Let us look historically at this law—Between 1999 and 2019; six general elections have been held, producing four (4) Presidents—Olusegun Obasanjo, Musa Yar'Adua, Goodluck Jonathan, and Muhammadu Buhari. A single political party (Peoples Democratic Party – PDP) has produced three of those Presidents from the first 4 elections (1999, 2003, 2007, and 2011) while another Party—All Progressive Congress produced one of those presidents from the 2015 and 2019 elections. No other party has come close to winning even one-tenth of the votes required.

According to the official results from INEC in 2019 Presidential election—the results of first five political parties for an election with 84 million registered voters, 91 registered political parties, and 71 Presidential candidates are:

- APC—15,191,847;

- PDP—11,262,978

- PCP—107,286

- ADC—97,874

- APGA—66,851

In terms of governorship, the PDP in 1999 started with 21 Governors and in 2007 has 27 governors out of the 36 States. Currently, they have about 19 states. The APC (a merger of ACN, ANPP, CPC, APGA, and disgruntled PDP members) currently have 18 Governors. In 2015, they have 21 governors.

No other political party except the PDP has governed these states – Abia, Adamawa, Akwa Ibom, Bayelsa, Cross River, Delta, Ebonyi, Enugu, Rivers, and Taraba. On the other hand, since 1999, APC (transformed from AD, AC, ACN) has governed Lagos through its comptroller in chief Tinubu and his protéges

Since 2003, after PDP won the election in 1999, Anambra state has not been governed by any other political party except APGA. On the other hand, Ondo state has been governed by LP from 2011 to 2019.

These reflect a continued dominance of mainstream political parties in wherever is their stronghold.

Nigerians are notoriously religious and the voting patterns will once again no doubt look very different in the predominantly Muslim north compared to some areas in the south where more Christians live.

—*Will Ross*

CHAPTER FIVE

FIFTH LAW

Ethnicity, religion are the major factors in Nigerian politics. If you are a Muslim, you'll have a certain appeal to Muslims, if you're a Christian the same thing will happen with Christians. Opponents will formulate all kinds of conspiracy theories to pit you against those who don't share the same creed or ethnic sentiments with you. Beware of that.

Even within your state, division is rife. If not from a Senatorial Zone to another, it will be between local governments, or different constituencies and wards. Even within the Christian religion, there's a division of denomination—Catholics, Anglican, Winners, Assemblies of God, Jehovah's Witnesses, etc. Or in Islam, it'll be a sort of Sectarian divisions: Sunni, Shia, Kharijite, Ibadi, Murji'ah. Each of these people will tend to have a certain type of affinity towards those that worship or come from the same place as they do. Often times, competence is relegated to the back door.

This response during every election is always the same: most Muslims queue behind Muslim candidates and Christians queue behind Christian candidates. The last thing anybody considers is the viewpoint and credibility of the candidates. We simply take sides along our prejudices and the politicians knowing this, fan the flame, leading to killings and kidnappings.

MURIC—Muslim Rights Concern and CAN—Christian Association of Nigeria (CAN) whip up these divisive sentiments for political gain. The North will normally resist a Southern Christian President. And the South view with suspicion a Northern Muslim President. It's noteworthy that a greater number of Muslims voted for Buhari over Jonathan or Obasanjo. A greater number of Christians voted too for Jonathan and Obasanjo over Buhari.

Let's look at Chidi Amuta intervention shortly, "As a fact of political reality, major religious organisations control and command large followership and in the process become politically consequential. Faith and its tremendous followership is a political force all over the world. Our political leadership make it a point of duty to either attend the Friday Muslim prayers or pay ceremonial visits to the enclaves of major Pentecostal churches as a way of enhancing their political followership. The political clout of religion becomes matrixed in the general calculus of democratic outcomes in times of electoral contest... More importantly, Nigeria is no ordinary place in matters of religion and faith. Our people breathe and live religion. People are either Moslems, Christians or superstitious animists steeped in the ancient covens of primordial origins. Somehow, obsessive religiosity has come to fill the vacant space left in the consciousness of our people by the absence of national loyalty and patriotic fervour. Either as Moslems or Christians, Nigerians are more likely to kill or die for their faith than for the nation. In recent times, the exploitation of religious differences by the presiding political leadership has weaponized the two dominant faiths into opposing armies with undisguised militancy.[14]

This was more apparent in the 2015 elections involving a Christian Southern President and a Muslim Northern candidate. Ethnic and religious sentiments played a major role. The sentiments emerged from the PDP's zoning arrangement for power to alternate between the geopolitical zones especially between the zones in the North and South of Nigeria. In 1999, power had been zoned to the South and was expected to return after eight years to the North. However, the administration of President Umaru Yar'Adua was short-lived as he died in office and was succeeded by the sitting Vice President, Goodluck Jonathan from the South. Being the incumbent in 2011, it was easy for President Goodluck Jonathan to pick his party's ticket.

But the North in 2015 was hell bent on getting back political power. The APC deliberately fielded a Northern Candidate and a lot of northern political stakeholders from the north decamped from the PDP to the APC, while most of them returned to the PDP when they fielded a Muslim candidate in the 2019 Presidential Elections.

Understand: Victory in Nigeria's elections has huge religious, and ethnic undertones. The ease with which both the Muslim council and Christian Association use its religious authority to play politics indicates religious mobilization for political gain in our polarized society. Unfortunately, when leaders fail to address problems such as poverty, underdevelopment, and youth unemployment, the usually fan the religious and ethnic emblem to distract people from the real issue of underdevelopment and poverty. You must learn to use this to your advantage. You must ensure that you develop a connection with the head of religious organizations – who are religious leaders with far reaching influence. You don't necessarily have to believe in their religious creed you only have to share the same vested interest in a mutually beneficial agenda. Keeping this alliance will serve you well in your political game.

If you are interested in Nigeria's Presidency, as much as you appeal to the public, assiduously court the right influencers, work behind the scenes to build trust with the ultimate decision makers.

— Ùgòchúkwú Àlòh

CHAPTER SIX

SIXTH LAW

Anyone who wants to succeed in Nigerian politics especially at the Presidency must be ready to Kowtow to at least 80 percent of the cabals including former Heads of State, a few revered monarchs, some Political Godfathers—Former Presidents and Governors—and some members of the private sector economic cabal—Aliko Dangote, Mike Adenuga Jr, Tony Elumelu, Jim Ovia, Abdulsamad Rabiu, Femi Otedola, Theophilus Danjuma, and others. Certainly, there are also foreign interests, particularly the United Kingdom, the United States of America, and China.

Electoral victory in Nigeria mostly depends on the support of "godfathers", also known as "cabals", to further improve one's chances at the polls. Don't be deceived when someone says godfatherism has been buried in Nigeria's politics. People have said that the recent re-election of

Godwin Obaseki as Governor of Edo State even when his APC godfathers abandoned him is a revelation of the end of Godfatherism in Nigerian politics. But such people are in for a rude awakening. APC political godfathers may have rejected Obaseki prior to the polls but he quickly found new political godfathers in PDP who deployed resources and practically relocated to the state to help him achieve victory. At best what happened in Edo Gubernatorial election was a change of godfathers not the end of godfatherism.

Most times, the cabals are so powerful that they are virtually responsible for the emergence of every successful candidate from whichever state they control. Alhaji Olusola Saraki, the father of former Senate President Bukola Saraki, reigned as godfather in Kwara state and almost always single-handedly determined who emerged for federal and state elections, from the state. One Godfather in Oyo state, once openly boasted to have sponsored every successful politician, including the governor and federal and state legislators.

Unfortunately, like all things in politics, getting the support of godfathers does not come cheap, whether in monetary terms, which have to be paid in advance, or through a commitment to regular returns of a percentage of certain budget lines of state resources. The godfathers are typically above the law and able to mobilize support, money, and violence for candidates. Disobeying them even while in the office can be brutal. Governor Ambode suffered this in Lagos State. In 2003, Governor Chris Ngige of Anambra state attracted the anger of his godfather Chris Uba when he reneged on terms of agreements after been sworn in as governor. Again, the impeachment of Governor Rashidi Ladoja of Oyo state in 2006 was facilitated by his godfather, Alhaji Lamidi Adedibu, as punishment for not paying him N15 million monthly from the state security budget.[15]

Understand: Nigeria is not like France where young dudes like Emmanuel Macron or America where Barack Obama came unexpectedly, took on the establishment with remarkable oratory, technology, charisma, and swayed millions of voters to believe in their message and support them to victory. Don't assume that since Nigeria youths constitute the majority of the voting population, they are tired of the cabals. Nigeria is simply not ready for that kind of politics. As a young contestant, use technology, use your intelligence, use your skills, but do not forget to try and court the favour of those who wield influence in your state. *Some people vote simply because certain people ask them to vote.*

If you are interested in Nigeria's Presidency, as much as you appeal to the public, assiduously court the right influencers, work behind the scenes to build trust with the ultimate decision-makers. You better make sure that you don't overemphasize giving rousing speeches to your supporters at the cost of shoring up relationships with critical allies. Developing or alienating the right relationships with the right people is indispensable to success in Nigeria's politics. This is how most elections are won and lost.

If you knew a thing about Nigerian elections, you just knew that violence plays a massive role in determining who comes out victorious and who loses.

—Goodluck Jonathan

CHAPTER SEVEN

SEVENTH LAW

If you must survive (not succeed), you have to be security conscious. In every election cycle, there is usually violence and bloodshed. The level of violence is directly proportional to the resolved willingness of violent politicians to take power by force. So even if you lose the election, endeavor not to lose your life. Be security conscious, play it safe, get your message to the people as much as you can.

Despite Nigeria's enormous resources, the majority of the youth under 30 years old are deeply impoverished, unemployed, and increasingly frustrated with violence. There are always a ready army of unemployed and unemployable youths willing to be manipulated by politicians to wreak havoc in elections.

Early on the morning of February 23rd, 2019, (the day for the Presidential Election) in my constituency, there was rainfall of gunshots, thugs of the two major parties APC versus those of PDP slug it out. This led to voters suppression and intimidation, as the thugs of the two major parties stuffed and thumb printed the ballot papers to their own satisfaction. Many electorates of my constituency didn't vote, I dared to go and vote amidst the violence and confronted those thugs who threatened to beat me up and destroyed my phone for trying to take pictures of their misdemeanors.

After the presidential election on Saturday, I resumed my campaign the next Monday. Most people I met made similar statements like: "I'll vote for you, if only they will allow us to vote this time around." (obviously referring to the incident of Feb 23rd). My response to them was that, "this time it's not going to be like that, the security agencies have taken note and will do their job". Little did I know that the worst was in stock.

On March 8, 2020, a day before the election, a group of thugs invaded the place where the electoral materials were stored in three wards of my constituency, they chased away INEC ad-hoc staffs and burnt the materials to ashes. Elections did not hold the following day. It had to be rescheduled later. That was a betrayal of democracy. A mockery to the sanctity of the ballot. After that, whenever I talked to people to come and vote on the rescheduled date, they told me plain no, that they won't risk their lives, that Nigeria is not worth it. In hindsight, it was revealed that the burnt electoral materials was a tactical ploy to scare away voters so that they hoodlums can have a field day on the rescheduled date.

The reality is that electoral violence is one of the strategies employed by Nigerian politicians during electioneering period. Desperate and power drunk politicians often sponsor unemployed youths and stark illiterates to carry out assaults on their perceived political opponents with a view to manipulating election results to their own advantage. [16]

The signing of peace accords by some politicians does not equate peaceful elections. After 2011 Nigeria General Elections, Human Rights Watch reported that about 800 lives were lost and more than 65,000 people were displaced.[17] The Nigerian Red Cross Society released a slightly lower figure indicating that the violence displaced 48,000 persons in 12 states.[18] In a similar fashion, the European Union Election Observation Mission reported that about 30 people were killed on April 11, 2015 Election Day as a result of inter-party clashes and attacks on election sites.

In 2015 about 100 deaths were recorded. According to INEC, there were 66 reports of violent incidence all across the country. The violence were recorded in Rivers State (16 incidents); Ondo (8);

Cross Rivers (6); Ebonyi (6); Akwa Ibom (5); Bayelsa (4); Lagos and Kaduna (3 each); Jigawa, Enugu, Ekiti (2 each); Katsina, Kogi, Plateau, Abia, Imo, Kano and Ogun (one each).[19]

Understand: *In every election cycle, the level of bloodshed is directly proportional to the level of violence and resolved willingness of violent politicians to take power by force.*

Victory most times is not determined by who the electorates chose but by those who outrigged the opponent in the rigging contest we call an election. Like I said in the introduction, the absence of meaningful governance has made Nigerians a government unto themselves as they provide their own infrastructures by generating electricity using personal generating sets; getting water by individually digging boreholes or wells, and employing personal security guards to ensure the safety of life and properties. So as a young politician, you also have to make personal provisions for security because there is no state security for you.

*Elsewhere, election results are supposed
to be a reflection of the will of the voters
but often in Nigeria the voters are
completely disregarded, their right to
vote negated and their will rendered
irrelevant. Instead, the will of one
presiding judge, sitting with subordinate
trusted judges, is substituted for the will
of the entire voting population which
may run into millions.*
— *Oserheimen Osunbor*

*It is not only elections that are rigged in
Nigeria, many judgements, especially on
election petition matters, are now also
traded.*
—*Segun Adeniyi*

CHAPTER EIGHT

EIGHT LAW

Elections in Nigeria do not end with the announcement of the result, the terminate in court rulings. Never assume that being announced winner by INEC means you have been elected; you have to be battle-ready for legal hassles. There's is an interesting intersection between politics and the court in Nigeria, but it did not start today.

According to the awesome journalist Olusegun Adeniyi, "On 14th June 1993, when the then National Electoral Commission (NEC) suspended the release of the results of the presidential election held two days earlier, in deference to a court injunction obtained by the Chief Arthur Nzeribe-led Association for Better

Nigeria (ABN). Following the development, there was a meeting at the then NICON-NOGA Hilton (now Transcorp) hotel where no fewer than six governors of the defunct Social Democratic Party (SDP) were gathered to deliberate on the next line of action.

"Right in my presence, three of the Governors, (two from South and another from the North) made calls to their respective states. While I had no idea about the people at the other end of the telephone lines, the instructions were very clear: they should go and meet Justice so, so and so to be granted order ex-parte to compel NEC to release the presidential election result. Looking back today, the real issue was not that the Governors wanted and got the court orders they requested but rather that each was specific as to which Judge whoever they were sending should go to. What that implies is that it is not all judges that are susceptible to such manipulation and corruption."[20]

In summary, Adeniyi wrote, "*it is not only elections that are rigged in Nigeria, many judgments, especially on election petition matters, are now also traded.*"

According to INEC, over 1,689 cases were filed in different courts in connection with the 2019 general election. The commission said about 890 of the cases were pre-election matters arising from the conduct of political party primary elections, while

799 were election petitions at the various tribunals across the country. Of the contested 1,490 federal and state legislative seats, about 776 (52.08%) were decided by the courts. Since the conclusion of the 2019 general election, INEC has been compelled by the courts to withdraw 121 certificates of return from winners and award them to someone else, including those who were not even on the ballot during the election. 91 of these cases were pre-election matters which arose principally from the conduct of party primaries, it is only in 28 cases that INEC was asked to withdraw certificates from the winners on account of issues arising from the elections.

No doubt, the law fully permitted electoral litigations. For example, Section 87, subsection 10 of the Electoral Act 2010 (as amended) states: "Notwithstanding the provisions of the Act or rules of a political party, an aspirant who complains that any of the provisions of this Act and the guidelines of a political party has not been complied with in the selection or nomination of a candidate of a political party for election, may apply to the Federal High Court or the High Court of a State, for redress."

Section 246 (3) of the 1999 Constitution (as amended) confers finality on the judgment of the Appeal Tribunal in legislative elections. But until 2011, gubernatorial elections ended at the Court of

Appeal. But after the ugly judicial fracas between then, CJN Justice Katsina Alu and the President of the Court of Appeal, Justice Ayo Salami over Sokoto State gubernatorial election matter, litigations for Governorship elections were extended to the Supreme Court. Today we have three phases of litigations for gubernatorial election: Tribunal, Appeal Tribunal, and the Supreme Court. For all other positions, including the presidency, there are only two phases of litigations.

In terms of the power of court judgements in Nigeria's modern political history, let us begin with Peter Obi. He contested in the Anambra State governorship election under the then-nascent political party, All Progressive Grand Alliance (APGA) in 2003 and won. His victory was, however, stolen by the rival PDP candidate Chris Ngige who was declared the winner by the Independent National Electoral Commission (INEC).

He went to court where he battled for three years before the Court of Appeal on 15 March 2006 ruled that Obi was the rightful winner of the election. Obi took office on 17 March 2006, but on 2 November 2006, after seven months in office, the PDP dominated State House of Assembly orchestrated a kangaroo impeachment against him, replacing him with his deputy Virginia Etiaba. Obi successfully challenged his impeachment and was re-instated as the governor on 9 February 2007 by the Court of Appeal again.[21]

After the 2007 general elections, Obi was chased out of the governor's office on 29 May 2007 by Andy Uba the presumptive winner of the election. Obi challenged such egregious election in the courts, this time contending that the four-year tenure he had won in the 2003 elections only started to run when he took office in March 2006. On 14 June 2007, the Supreme Court nullified Andy Uba's election on the grounds that Obi's four-year tenure should have remained undisturbed until March 2010. This returned Obi to office for the remainder of his term and second term which he won successfully.

On October 25, 2007, the Nigerian Supreme Court unilaterally sacked an elected governor, Celestine Omehia, and installed an unelected individual Mr. Rotimi Amaechi who did not participate in the Rivers State governorship election as the duly elected governor of the state. In contrast to Obi's case who participated but was robbed of his mandate, the Supreme court in a unanimous decision, said Amaechi was wrongly substituted by the Peoples Democratic Party (PDP) and that the indictment on which his disqualification was anchored in was unlawful. The court consequently held that Amaechi was PDP's governorship standard-bearer in the said election.

According to Justice George Oguntade who read the lead judgement, Section 221 of the 1999 Constitution provides: "No association other than a political party shall canvass for votes for any candidate in any election or contribute to the funds of any party or to the election expenses of any candidate in an election."

"The above provision effectually removes the possibility of independent candidacy in our elections; and places emphasis and responsibility in elections on political parties. Without a political party, a candidate cannot contest. The primary method of contest for elective offices is therefore between the parties. If as provided in Section 221 above, it is a party that canvasses for votes, it follows that it is a party that wins an election. A good or bad candidate may enhance or diminish the prospect of his party in winning but at the end of the day, it is the party that wins or loses in election."[22] Oguntade added.

Based on this judgement, APC comfortably substituted Prince Abubakar Audu who died during the election (on 22nd November 2015) with Yahaya Bello, before the conduct of the supplementary election. Of course, it was a heinous injustice to Hon. Faleke who was Abubakar Audu deputy in the Kogi Governorship election of 2015. Both the courts and INEC upheld APC's choice.

On July, 5, 2019, The Supreme Court decided on the Osun State governorship election between Ademola Adeleke of the PDP and Adegboyega Oyetola of the APC by relying solely on technicalities to dismiss the appeal filed by Adeleke. The court ruled that the absence, during a previous sitting of Justice Peter Obiorah, who read the election tribunal's majority judgment declaring Adeleke of the PDP winner, nullified the tribunal's judgment. Even for an action that was not of Adeleke's making, he was denied his mandate based on technicalities.

On May 24, 2019, The Supreme Court voided the votes of the All Progressives Congress members, elected in Zamfara State for different positions, on the basis that they were not duly nominated. The court, in a decision made by a five-member panel, ruled that there were no primaries conducted in Zamfara State by the APC and that the party could therefore not have emerged winner in any of the state elections.

According to the judgement read by Justice Paul Galinje, the apex court said the APC "could not have won the elections since it had no valid candidates in the said polls…The lower court was right to hold that there were no valid elections conducted in Zamfara State. A party that had no candidate cannot be said to have won an election," Mr. Galinje said while reading the judgment.

On January 14, 2020, the Supreme Court delivered its most controversial verdict yet in this democratic dispensation. In the unanimous judgment of the seven-member panel, read by Justice Kudirat Kekere-Ekun, the apex court agreed that results in 388 polling units were unlawfully excluded during the collation of the final governorship election result in Imo State. Justice Kekere-Ekun said with the results from the 388 polling units added, Mr. Uzodinma polled a majority of the lawful votes and ought to have been declared the winner of the election by the Independent National Electoral Commission, INEC.

Consequently, she set aside the declaration of Mr Ihedioha as the winner of the 2019 governorship election in Imo state and ordered that the certificate of return wrongly or unlawfully issued to Mr Ihedioha be immediately withdrawn by INEC and a fresh one issued to Mr. Uzodinma as the elected governor of the state.[23]

It was a betrayal of democracy. A daylight robbery of someone's mandate using the court as the tool. As Journalist Simon Kolawole puts it, "the apex court set tongues on fire. Protesters hit the streets, commentators spat venom and politicians cried blue murder over the verdict. The consensus among those opposed to the judgment is that the Supreme Court miscarried justice."

On February 13, 2020, less than 24 hours to the swearing-in of APC's David Lyon as the governor, the Supreme court nullified his election because of the credentials of Senator Biobarakuma Degi-Eremienyo, the deputy governor-elect. The two-time senator was accused of providing "false information" and swearing to an affidavit to back his claims in the nomination forms submitted to the Independent National Electoral Commission (INEC). Since his candidature was nullified, that also meant Lyon, his principal, suffered the collateral damage. Both of them had to go down together.[24]

In total, about four governors—Chris Ngige, Celestine Omehia, Emeka Ihedioha, and some may add David Lyon have been sacked by the Supreme Court since the 4th Republic.

The situation is not different from NASS, there are ample examples to cite of how the court has sacked, replaced, or suspended several of its members. Following his defeat by Dr. Datti Baba-Ahmed at the 2011 general election, former Kaduna State Governor and then Senator representing Kaduna North Senatorial District, Ahmed Mohammed Makarfi, approached the Tribunal. Alleging ballot stuffing, use of fake, unsigned, and unstamped ballot papers among other malpractices, Makarfi asked the tribunal for a recount of the ballot papers, and his wish was granted. In the end,

Makarfi was declared the winner with the majority of lawful votes of 364,801 against Baba-Ahmed's 356,579 votes. Despite the fact that the Tribunal played the role of INEC in that case, when the defeated gubernatorial candidate of the defunct Congress for Progressive Change (CPC), Mr. Haruna Saeed Kajuru asked for a recount of the votes in the keenly contested election, the same tribunal dismissed his petition.

Yet another questionable election case is that of how Dino Melaye who was bundled out of the Senate based on a clerical error that had nothing to do with the result. Instead of 23rd February when the election was conducted, the returning officer wrote 25th February, the day the result was declared. When Melaye's lawyer asked the appeal tribunal to tally the figures as proof that the result was genuine, the Judges said it was not their responsibility to be doing INEC job. The election was nullified on that basis.[25]

In such infamous vein, Courts of coordinate jurisdiction have continued to make a mockery of the rule of law in the tussle for the Anambra South Senatorial seat by the trio of Chris Uba, Ifeanyi Uba, and Obinna Uzor. In the election of February last year, Ifeanyi Uba of the Young Progressives Party (YPP) was declared the winner while the defeated Chris Uba of the PDP petitioned the tribunal where he lost. The appeal tribunal also dismissed his petition. But Chris Uba and Obinna Uzor (who claims to have won the PDP ticket) have secured separate judgements in Abuja to throw Ifeanyi Uba out of the Senate, on account of the allegation that he forged his NECO certificate.[26]

Looking at all these together, on 16th March 2016, INEC Chairman, Prof. Mahmood Yakubu, once lamented of this judicial rascality when he complained: "The Court of Appeal, in one judicial division, ordered INEC to conduct fresh election 'in which only the duly qualified candidates shall participate'. In another division, the Court of Appeal, under similar circumstances, nullified the election, disqualified the candidate, and allowed the political party to submit the name of another candidate for the re-run election. Yet in another division, the Court of Appeal nullified the election and ordered INEC to conduct a fresh election but is silent about the status of the disqualified candidate, thereby giving room for endless commentary and new rounds of litigation on the eligibility of the disqualified candidate to participate in re-run elections."[27]

Doubtless, many people have pointed out the inherent danger staring us in the face when judges become electors of candidates. And have called for reforms to put an end to judges electing candidates. For example, Prof. Oserheimen Osunbor as Chairman of the Nigerian Law Reform

Commission (NLRC), argued, "Elsewhere, election results are supposed to be a reflection of the will of the voters but often in Nigeria the voters are completely disregarded, their right to vote negated and their will rendered irrelevant. Instead, the will of one presiding judge, sitting with subordinate trusted judges, is substituted for the will of the entire voting population which may run into millions. There is obviously something intrinsically wrong with this practice and it may, if left unchecked, have grave security and other consequences for the judiciary, a state, or even the country as a whole in future."[28]

Former President Goodluck Jonathan recounted a meeting he had with the leadership of both the National Assembly and the judiciary on how to find an institutional framework in the bid to combat corruption in our country. In his own words: "...I also invited Chief Judges from one state in each of the six geopolitical zones. I specifically requested for Lagos and Anambra to represent their zones. My choosing Anambra was because that is one state where every political aspirant goes into election with at least two court orders in his pocket. You cannot fight corruption without dealing with such issues".[29]

Mr. Femi Falana, a Senior Advocate of Nigeria (SAN), in an interview on Arise News Channel, held that the judiciary's role in adjudicating or determining the outcome of elections in this country should be kept to the barest minimum because judges are not suited to determine the winners of elections. That, according to Falana, is the exclusive preserve of the electorate. For him, there are no provisions in the courtroom to determine the winners of elections.

Segun Adeniyi sentiment is equally apt in this matter. In his article titled 'When Judges Imperil Democracy', he said: "At all times and in all circumstances, the role of the courts as the interpreter of the law, resolver of disputes and defender of the Constitution, requires that Judges abide by their oath. That explains why a judiciary debilitated by, or prone to, all manner of misconduct, including corruption and political interference, is a danger to society. Sadly, we can see the evidence of this in our polity and it is important for critical stakeholders to understand that we cannot continue like this if our nation must develop and thrive. The judiciary is enmeshed in a sordid dance of shame that appears to defy all the known rules of engagement in our fledgling democracy...by offering themselves as willing tools for desperate politicians.[30]

Understand: it is important that you as a political contestant know that one of the most basic qualities of leadership— integrity is lacking in the majority of the men and women in leadership positions across the country – in executive, judiciary, legislature, and the generality of the public sector. And that most times the electorate do not have the final say in electoral results but the court. *The reality as Adeniyi said is that not only elections that are rigged in Nigeria, many judgements, especially on election petition matters, are now also traded.* And so until the electoral system is reformed nay revolutionized, to minimize the determination of election by judges, always gear yourself for a legal battle.[31]

A WORD TO THE NIGERIAN YOUTH

HAVING NOW COME TO THE END of this outline and incomplete review of the laws of Nigerian politics, it will be well to consider, in conclusion, the necessity of the youths in the political process. Historically, the youths are the active conscience of any country and that is why they are the ones usually engaged in activism for civil rights, justice, equity, and freedom.

There are no reasons Nigerian youths are to become exceptions. There's no reason a Nigerian youth should agree to be used for thuggery, ballot box snatching, or burning. There is no reason why Nigerian youths should not be able to form a coalition of genuine civil societies to demand serious accountability from their leaders. There is nothing that stops the youth from demanding respect for the dignity of all Nigerians—old and young alike no matter their gender, tribe, religion, status, ability, or disability. There is no reason the Nigerian youths should not seek justice for the oppressed and demand reforms in the judicial sector. There is no reason Nigeria youths should not fight for freedom of worship, schooling, and trading and for any Nigerian to pursue his/her dreams in any part of the country without inhibition/restrictions, ethnicism, fear of rejection, hate, violence, or even death. The recent dissolution of the Special Anti-Robbery Squad (SARS) shows the power of the youths when they make demand on how they should be governed. For years the abuse of power by the SARS personnel have progressively worsened in a manner that degrades, endangers and threaten the life and other fundamental human rights of citizens. But with the youths protesting in the streets and social media platforms, the demand became global and went viral. And the presidency has no other option but to capitulate to the demands of the youths. Yet I believe that the Nigerian youths can still do more.

This is because the youthful age is a period of education not ignorance; a period of innovation not destruction; a period of dignifying life not destroying it, a period of creativity and entrepreneurship not dormancy or degeneration.

According to the statistics released by INEC with regard to the list of 84 million registered voters, 80% representing 68 million voters are youths. In fact, between ages (18 - 35) we have 51.11% representing 42,938,458 voters. Let us use our numerical strength and youthfulness to remove these political charlatans that are liabilities to our State and blockages to our development. I'll advise the youths never again to vote because of money, never to sell their vote for rice, T-shirts, because N1,000 gotten before or during election won't give you job or light, or road or water for four years. Just like Omoyele Sowore said, those who betrayed your past and continue to compromise your present cannot guarantee your future.

The number of jobless Nigerian youths has grown progressively over the last 20 years. Data from the National Bureau of Statistics reveals Nigeria's unemployment rate as of the second quarter of 2020 is 27.1% indicating that about 21,764,614 (21.7 million) Nigerians remain unemployed, while the underemployment rate is (28.6%). This means the total number of Nigerians who are unemployed or underemployed as of 2020 Q2 is 55.7%.

Most of our youths will not be beggars or criminals today, if they had education/vocational skills, economic opportunities, funding, security, social infrastructure, and responsible leadership and good societal role models in the last 20 years.

Therefore, to every Nigerian youths I say: we must prepare to take back our country from the hands of the cabals as future generation awaits our prowess. The survival of tomorrow is based on the actions and decisions of today's youths. I believe Nigerian politics can be upgraded and rescued if we all summon the courage to get involved in it. For history is made by those who stare at impossibility in the face and strive to sterilize it.

But as I have consistently maintained in various posts in my blog: Sirpeteraloh.com and posts on social media, the chief cause of failure in leadership is the desire to serve oneself rather than others. Any leader who serves himself instead of the common good is already displaying his certificate of incompetence. Successive administrations in Nigeria has shown nothing but mockery for leadership, and a travesty of governance tottering to an unidentifiable terminus a quo with impotent and selfish captains.

But one thing I like is that these are the very springs and fountains of revolution. The youth have been marginalized for too long which makes you wonder where the future of the future leaders lies. Too often, the youth is at the peripheral of their policymaking (if there is any at all), almost of no consequence, except maybe as a nuisance, an object to steal votes and hunt down political enemies who they will pop champagne with when they meet in the social club of the elites.

Fortunately, history is the most important drama of all times, and the "signs of the times" show that we stand at a critical moment in the

"Nigerian drama". The youth have played so long to the script drafted by these buccaneers, philanderers, and profiteers. The passage of the NTYTR ACT has given us an expansion of choice. A choice to press forward with a better model of governance rooted in transparency and accountability, true democracy, and respect for human rights or to allow these corrupt politicians to steal our future while dividing us along age-old lines of ethnic identities, sects, movements, tribes, and religious affiliations.

I suggest that we should choose the former. This is no longer the time to see politics as part of the problem, but as part of the solution. Let us not subscribe to the cynicism and distrust that sees politics as a dirty game; that sees election as politics as usual. Now is the time to refocus politics on what it should be—the search for the common good. Our responsibilities range from building active civil society organizations that hold politicians accountable or running for office to understanding issues and assessing candidate's qualifications and positions on key issues, voting for credible candidates while jettisoning all pursuit of partisan advantage, vote selling or thuggery, ballot box snatching, and violence.

It's the duty of the youths to measure every party based on how much their agenda furthers excellence in human life, love, freedom, truth, and the pursuit of happiness. The fundamental question should be: where is the "least among us" in your policy framework? Where's that beggar at Abakpa main market Abakaliki in your agenda? Where's that Kano's disadvantaged child who's the victim of irresponsible parenthood in your policy? Where is that Lagos unemployed graduate roaming endlessly carrying files and CV in your program? And stuffs like that.

Ultimately, it is how well we're able to manage the country's most precious resources - "the poor in our midst" that will determine the success of any developmental paradigm orchestrated anywhere either in Abuja or in Abakaliki.

What I'm humbly, gently, enthusiastically, and lovingly suggesting is that if you want to partake in Nigeria politics and to a great extent those of third world countries, then utilize these laws backed up with your good intentions. And— when the time comes for you to utilize power, devote it to improving the lives of the people, make sure that no one is left behind.

I'm confident that the laws in this book chart the best pathway to success in Nigeria politics— even though, as with so many things in life, I can offer no guarantees. Regardless, I take great comfort and pride in the knowledge that you are now fully prepared to make your voice count and achieve victory.

World productivity expert Robin Sharma spent over four years studying the potency of rising early in the morning and the impact on human productivity. In recording his findings in one of his books, the 5 am club, one of the students of the club asked, "What if I only want to do these five days a week and take weekends off? How strict is this whole 5 AM Method?"

It was Sharma's response that I want to end with: "It's your life. Do what fits you best and feels right to you. What I'm revealing is the information…Apply it all in whatever way works for your values, aspirations, and lifestyle. Yet also know that part-time commitment truly does deliver part-time results"

Ok, dear political aspirant, I have a strong list of learning and action resources that will help you thrive and rise in Nigerian politics without having to go through the most difficult hurdles.

I know they will serve you well:
My free ebook on POLITICS 101
My free REGULAR POLITICAL POSTS ON sirpeteraloh.com

And to completely wow you…

I am pleased to announce to you my new course UNDERSTANDING AND PLAYING NIGERIAN POLITICS dedicated to you.

Having studied political philosophy with a double degree from both Urban University, Rome and Imo State University Owerri, I proceeded to acquire multiple learning resources and certificates from Yale University and Stanford University, I've distilled the best strategies, findings, and philosophies into an actionable program that will enable you to strategically position yourself to contest and win elections in Nigeria and do enormous good residing deep in your heart. Like it or not, the world recognizes you for what you do, not what's in your heart.

You're the person Nigeria is waiting for to become its beacon of light in the African Continent. Africa can easily become the leading continent in science, technology, green energy, Artificial Intelligence, economic growth, etc., if only she has leaders who know what she possesses and can deploy the necessary resources to launch her on a global scale.

Yet to do something extremely special for upcoming politicians to succeed, when you register for my course, I'll completely share with you my notebooks, textbooks, and numerous learning tools from my professors and mentors...and the perennial lessons I learned from running as the youngest political candidate in my state Ebonyi in the state legislative assembly in 2019...with their permission.

The best way to play a game successfully is to know the rules detailedly so that you can bend it to your favour. So get off the fence and go ahead and get full access by sending me an email: Sirpeteraloh@gmail.com.

REFERENCES

Amuta, Chidi. "Who Regulates the Political Industry?" *Thisday* , 10 May 2020, www.thisdaylive.com/index.php/2020/05/10/who-regulates-the-political-industry/.

[2] Snyder, Timothy. *On Tyranny: Twenty Lessons from the Twentieth Century*. The Bodley Head, 2017.

[3] Abati, Reuben. "Nigeria 2019: Notes from the Field," March 12, 2019. https://www.thisdaylive.com/index.php/2019/03/12/nigeria-2019-notes-from-the-field/.

[4] Moghalu , Kingsley. "Reflections on the 2019 Elections." *Nigerian Current*, 5 Apr. 2019, nigeriancurrent.com/2019/04/05/reflections-on-the-2019-elections-by-kingsley-moghalu/.

[5] Onyekpere, Eze. "Still Above the Ceiling (A Report on Campaign Finance and Use of State Administrative Resources in the 2015 Presidential Election)." Centre For Social Justice, 2015. http://csj-ng.org/wp-content/uploads/2018/06/Still-Above-the-Ceiling-_2015-Presidential-Campaign-Finance-Report_.pdf.

[6] Onyekpere, Eze. "Still Above the Ceiling (A Report on Campaign Finance and Use of State Administrative Resources in the 2015 Presidential Election)." Centre For Social Justice, 2015. http://csj-ng.org/wp-content/uploads/2018/06/Still-Above-the-Ceiling-_2015-Presidential-Campaign-Finance-Report_.pdf.

[7] Fabiyi, Olusola, Chukwudi Akasike, Ihuoma Chiedozie, and Simon Utebor, eds. "Presidential Primary: Dollar Rain as Saraki, Atiku, Tambuwal Divide PDP Leaders." Punch Newspapers, October 7, 2018. https://punchng.com/dollar-rain-as-saraki-atiku-tambuwal-divide-pdp-leaders/.

[8] Onyekpere, Eze. "Still Above the Ceiling (A Report on Campaign Finance and Use of State Administrative Resources in the 2015 Presidential Election)." Centre For Social Justice, 2015. http://csj-ng.org/wp-content/uploads/2018/06/Still-Above-the-Ceiling-_2015-Presidential-Campaign-Finance-Report_.pdf.

[9] Abati, Reuben. "2019: A Brief Manual of Nigerian Politics." THISDAYLIVE, September 11, 2018. https://www.thisdaylive.com/index.php/2018/09/11/2019-a-brief-manual-of-nigerian-politics/.

[10] Abati, Reuben. "Nigeria 2019: Notes from the Field," March 12, 2019. https://www.thisdaylive.com/index.php/2019/03/12/nigeria-2019-notes-from-the-field/.

[11] Douglass, Frederick. *My Bondage, My Freedom*. Lanham, Chicago: Start Publishing LLC, 2013.

12 Moghalu , Kingsley. "Reflections on the 2019 Elections." *Nigerian Current*, 5 Apr. 2019, nigeriancurrent.com/2019/04/05/reflections-on-the-2019-elections-by-kingsley-moghalu/.

13 Abati, Reuben. "Nigeria 2019: Have We Learnt Any Lessons?" THISDAYLIVE, March 26, 2019. https://www.thisdaylive.com/index.php/2019/03/26/nigeria-2019-have-we-learnt-any-lessons/.

14 Amuta, Chidi. "Faith, Iniquity and the State." THISDAYLIVE, September 6, 2020. https://www.thisdaylive.com/index.php/2020/09/06/faith-iniquity-and-the-state/.

15 Olorunmola, Adebowale. "Cost Of Politics In Nigeria," 2015. https://www.wfd.org/wp-content/uploads/2017/09/Cost-of-Politics-Nigeria.pdf.

16 Olowojolu Olakunle et al., Trends in Electoral Violence in Nigeria. J. of Social Sciences and Public Policy, 2019, Vol. 11, Number 1, Pp. 37-52

17 Human Rights Watch., Nigeria: Post-Election Violence Killed 800., 2011, Washington DC: Human Rights Watch http://www.hrw.org/news/2011/05/16/nigeria-post-electionviolence-killed-800

18 Omenazu, E. and Paschal, N. 'Nigerians Displaced Polls Violence-Red Cross', Daily Independent (Lagos), 21 April. 2011.

19 (Vanguard, April 12, 2015).

[20] Olusegun Adeniyi "Judicial Black Market: Anambra as
Case Study." NewsWireNGR, March 17, 2016.
https://newswirengr.com/2016/03/17/olusegun-
adeniyi-judicial-black-market-anambra-as-case-
study/.

[21] "Peter Obi," Wikipedia (Wikimedia Foundation, August
21, 2020), https://en.wikipedia.org/wiki/Peter_Obi.
[22] Kennedy Emetulu, "Death, Inconclusive Election and
Law (II)," Blueprint Newspapers Limited, November 24,
2015, https://www.blueprint.ng/death-inconclusive-
election-and-law-ii/.

[23] Yahaya, Halima. "Why Supreme Court Sacked Ihedioha,
Declared APC's Uzodinma Winner." Premium Times
Nigeria, January 15, 2020.
https://www.premiumtimesng.com/news/headlines/
372652-why-supreme-court-sacked-ihedioha-declared-
apcs-uzodinma-winner-in-imo.html.

[24] Kolawole, Simon. "Supreme Court And The Bayelsa
Bombshell -By Simon Kolawole." Opinion Nigeria,
February 16, 2020.
https://www.opinionnigeria.com/supreme-court-and-
the-bayelsa-bombshell-by-simon-kolawole/).

[25] Segun Adeniyi , "When Judges Become Our Electoral
College," THISDAYLIVE, February 27, 2020,
https://www.thisdaylive.com/index.php/2020/02/27/whe
n-judges-become-our-electoral-college/.
[26] Segun Adeniyi , "When Judges Become Our Electoral
College," THISDAYLIVE, February 27, 2020,
https://www.thisdaylive.com/index.php/2020/02/27/whe
n-judges-become-our-electoral-college/.

[27] "INEC Boss Laments Conflicting Judgments in Election Cases," Punch Newspapers, March 17, 2016, https://punchng.com/inec-boss-laments-conflicting-judgments-in-election-cases/.

[28] Shaka Momodu, "Nigeria's Confounded Judiciary," THISDAYLIVE, September 23, 2019, https://www.thisdaylive.com/index.php/2019/09/23/nigerias-confounded-judiciary/.

[29] Adeniyi, Olusegun. *Against the Run of Play: How an Incumbent President Was Defeated in Nigeria*, 207. Lagos: Kachifo, 2017.

[30] Adeniyi, Olusegun. "Judicial Black Market: Anambra as Case Study." NewsWireNGR, March 17, 2016. https://newswirengr.com/2016/03/17/olusegun-adeniyi-judicial-black-market-anambra-as-case-study/.

[31] Momodu, Shaka. "Nigeria's Confounded Judiciary," September 23, 2019. https://www.thisdaylive.com/index.php/2019/09/23/nigerias-confounded-judiciary/.

Further Reading

Awolowo, Obafemi, *Thoughts on Nigerian Constitution*, Ibadan: Oxford University Press, 1966.

Azikiwe, N., *Renascent African*, London: Frank Can & Co., 1937.

Chinua Achebe, *The Trouble With Nigeria*

Obama, Barack, *The Audacity Of Hope: Thoughts On Reclaiming The American Dream*, New York: Crown Publishing Group, 2006.

Obama, Barack, *In a Promised Land*?

King, M. L. Jr. *Why We Can't Wait,* New York: Mentor Books, 1964

Segun Adeniyi, Against the Run of Play: How an Incumbent President Was Defeated in Nigeria

Segun Adeniyi, Power, Politics and Death: A front-row account of Nigeria under the late President Yar'Adua.Goodluck Jonathan, My Transition Hours

Ùgòchúkwú Àlòh, *Conquest of Limitations: Eliminating Waste of Resources for Nigeria's Development?*